Usborne Beginners
How flowe

D0865957

Emma Helbrough
Designed by Catherine-Anne MacKinnon
and Laura Parker

Illustrated by Maggie Silver and Uwe Mayer

Flower consultant: Dr. Margaret Rostron

Reading consultant: Alison Kelly
Roehampton University of Surrey

Contents

Lots of flowers

There are thousands of different kinds of flowers growing all over the world.

These amazing flowers are passion flowers.

Seeds to seedlings

A seed has a hard shell with a young plant inside. Seeds grow in the soil when the sun and rain has made them warm and wet.

These are sunflower seeds.

Each sunflower seed can grow into a big sunflower.

In the soil,
the shell of
a seed splits.

A small
root sprouts
out of it.

Then a shoot
grows out of
the seed.

When a shoot breaks
through the soil, it is
called a seedling.

The largest seed in the world is the
coco de mer. It is bigger than a football.

Plant parts

Most plants are made up of flowers, leaves, roots and stems.

This is a wood sorrel plant.

The stems keep the plant upright. Leaves and flowers grow on the stems.

Plants make food in their green leaves.

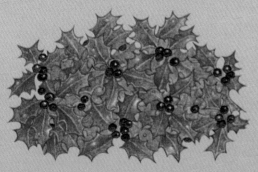

Some plants have leaves that are sharp and spiky.

They grow well as animals prefer to eat smooth leaves.

Lots of things you eat are plant parts. Broccoli is a bunch of flowers and carrots are a kind of root.

Underground, the roots soak up water from the soil. They hold the plant in place too.

Making food

Plants need food to grow. They use sunlight, air and water to make their food.

The leaves soak up air and sunlight.

Then the leaves suck rainwater up the stem from the roots.

The water, sunlight and air make food in the leaves.

8

Hyacinth   Tulip   Bluebell   Amaryllis

Some plants store their food in bulbs, which are made up of layers of special leaves.

Onions are a type of bulb. If you cut one in half, you can see its layers.

Buds to flowers

When a seedling has grown into a strong plant, it is ready to grow flowers.

Baby flowers are called buds.

The petals are tightly packed inside a bud.

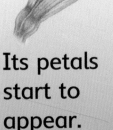

Slowly a bud begins to open.

Its petals start to appear.

The petals open into a flower.

Stamen

In the middle of a flower there are long tubes called stamens.

On the tips of the stamens there is some powder called pollen. Plants use pollen to make seeds.

Edelweiss flowers grow in cold places. They have a fluffy coat of hairs to keep them warm.

Pollen and nectar

Inside a flower there is a sweet juice called nectar. As insects and birds drink nectar, they take pollen from one flower to another.

When a bee drinks nectar, pollen sticks to its furry body.

It flies to another flower of the same kind and some of the pollen drops off.

This flower now has some pollen from another flower.

Pollen can rub onto a hummingbird's beak as it drinks nectar.

The pollen rubs off onto the next flower that the hummingbird visits.

Bees can collect nectar from over 1,000 flowers before they feel full!

Making seeds

Plants start to grow seeds as soon as they have some pollen from another plant.

When pollen lands on a poppy, a pod grows in the middle.

Seeds grow inside the pod and the flower begins to die.

The petals fall off, leaving a pod full of seeds.

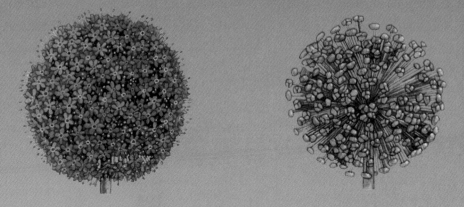

Alliums are made up of lots of tiny flowers.

Each flower becomes a tiny seed pod.

Chinese lantern seeds grow inside a hollow case.

Some caterpillars live in seed pods. When the caterpillars move, the pods seem to 'jump'.

Spreading seeds

Seeds need lots of space to grow, so they have to be scattered far apart.

Burdock seeds
have sharp,
spiky hooks.

They get caught on
an animal's fur as
it brushes past.

When the animal
scratches, the
seeds fall off.

Seed
pod

Crane's bill plants
have seed pods on
thin stems.

The stems curl up
and shoot the seeds
out of their pods.

Dandelion seeds
float on the wind
like little parachutes.

When ants carry seeds into their nests to
eat, some of the seeds begin to grow.

Juicy fruit

Some seeds grow inside fruit, berries and nuts. These seeds are spread by birds and animals.

When birds eat fruit and berries, they eat the seeds too.

They fly away and the seeds are spread in their droppings.

There are about 100 seeds inside every blueberry.

Chipmunks
eat fruit
and nuts.

They take their food into their burrows to
eat. The seeds are spread in their droppings.

Squirrels often bury
nuts in the ground
to eat later.

Then they forget
about them and the
seeds start to grow.

New plants

Some plants have special ways to make new plants.

Runner

A shoot called a runner grows out sideways from a strawberry plant.

When it touches the ground it grows roots.

A new plant grows from the roots and the runner rots away.

A small, new bulb grows on the side of a daffodil bulb.

The new bulb grows bigger and the two bulbs split apart.

Only one or two flowers grow from each daffodil bulb.

Rainforest flowers

Rainforests are warm, wet places. Trees block out sunlight, so it's dark on the ground.

Leaf hook

The leaves of glory lilies hook onto trees, so they can grow up to the sunlight.

Tank plants trap rainwater in their leaves. Frogs live in the pools of water.

A rafflesia
bud grows on
the ground.

It grows as
big as a
cabbage.

Its five red
petals start
to unfold.

Rafflesia flowers are as big as the wheels
on a truck and have no leaves or stems.

They smell of rotting meat to attract flies
which spread their pollen.

Hot deserts

Flowers even grow in hot, dry deserts.

Some desert plants don't grow while the soil is dry, but their seeds lie in the ground.

After rain, the seeds grow quickly into flowers.

The flowers make seeds and then die.

The new seeds will grow when it rains again.

Old man cactus plants are covered in woolly hair to shade them from the sun.

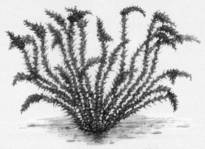

When it is dry the leaves fall off an ocotillo plant.

New leaves will grow again after it has rained.

Aloe plants store water inside their thick, spiky leaves.

Water plants

Some plants grow in ponds and lakes.

Many have roots which grow on the bottom of a lake.

Some water plants have roots which float in water.

A water lily's flowers float on the surface, so that insects can reach the pollen.

Most water plants don't grow in rivers, because they would be washed away.

Water lilies have flat leaves with a waxy surface. This helps them to float.

They don't sink even if a frog sits on them.

27

Killer plants

Some plants catch insects and turn them into juice, which they soak up.

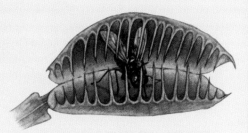

A fly lands in a Venus flytrap's spiky leaves.

The trap snaps shut and the fly slowly rots inside.

Sundew plants have sticky hairs which trap insects.

Pitcher plants have leaves which look like cups and are filled with water.

There is some nectar on the rim.

Ants crawl into pitcher plants to look for more nectar.

They slide into the water and drown. Then they rot.

Monkeys like to pick pitcher plants and drink the water inside.

29

Glossary of flower words

Here are some of the words in this book you might not know. This page tells you what they mean.

 seed - a hard shell with a young plant inside.

 seed pod - the part of a flower where the seeds grow.

 bulb - special underground leaves where some plants store their food.

 stamens - long tubes in the middle of a flower where pollen is made.

 pollen - a powder which plants swap with other plants to make seeds.

 nectar - a sweet juice inside flowers which animals, birds and insects drink.

 runner - a special stem which grows out sideways from some plants.

Web sites to visit

If you have a computer, you can find out more about how flowers grow on the Internet. On the Usborne Quicklinks Web site there are links to four fun Web sites.

Web site 1 - Find out which parts of plants you eat.

Web site 2 - Create a garden full of flowers then print the picture.

Web site 3 - Play a matching game and try to match the pairs of plants.

Web site 4 - Print a flower picture to fill in.

To visit these Web sites, go to **www.usborne-quicklinks.com** and type the keywords "beginners flowers". Then, click on the link for the Web site you want to visit. Before you use the Internet, look at the safety guidelines inside the back cover of this book and ask an adult to read them with you.

Index

Acknowledgements

Managing editor: Fiona Watt, Managing designer: Mary Cartwright

Photo credits

The publishers are grateful to the following for permission to reproduce material:
© **Alamy:** 5 (Bob Challinor/The Garden Picture Library), 9 (Angela Nicholson), 21 (Frank Krahmer/ImageState); © **Bruce Coleman:** 6-7 (Jorg & Petra Wagner), 28 (Kim Taylor); © **Corbis:** 2-3 (Chris Demetriou/Frank Lane Picture Agency), 10 (Darrell Gulin), 15 (Michelle Garrett); © **Digital Vision:** 4, 22; © **Frank Lane Picture Agency:** 29 (Mark Moffett/Minden Pictures); © **Getty:** 1 (Bruce Heinemann), 11 (Gary Braasch), 18 (Richard H Johnston), 31 (JH Pete Carmichael); © **Lost World Arts:** 23 (Karl Lehmann); © **Natural Visions:** 26-27 (Heather Angel); © **NHPA:** 25 (Patrick Fagot); © **Oxford Scientific Films:** Cover (Lightworker/gardenIMAGE), 13 (Michael Fogden); © **Robert Harding:** 14; © **Science Photo Library:** 17 (Lynwood Chase); © **Team Husar:** 19 (Lisa & Mike Husar). With thanks to Simon Gladding.